Here are some other DK Readers you might enjoy.

Level 1

LEGO® DC Universe™ Super Heroes: Ready for Action!
Watch out, super-villains! Batman™ and his fellow super heroes are here to save the day!

LEGO® Pirates: Brickbeard's Treasure
Join Captain Brickbeard and his pirate crew as they hunt for treasure on the high seas!

Level 2

The LEGO® Movie: Awesome Adventures
Meet Emmet and join him on his extraordinary quest to save the universe!

LEGO® Chima™: Tribes of Chima
Friend or Foe? Meet the amazing animal tribes of Chima™ and discover their fearsome weapons!

LEGO® Hero Factory: Brain Attack!
Hero Factory is under attack from an army of evil Brains. Can the robot heroes stop them?

LEGO® DC Universe™ Super Heroes: Super-Villains
POW! WHAM! Enter the dark and dangerous world of the planet's most feared super-villains.

A Note to Parents

DK READERS is a compelling program for beginning readers, designed in conjunction with leading literacy experts, including Dr. Linda Gambrell, Distinguished Professor of Education at Clemson University. Dr. Gambrell has served as President of the National Reading Conference, the College Reading Association, and the International Reading Association.

Beautiful illustrations and superb full-color photographs combine with engaging, easy-to-read stories to offer a fresh approach to each subject in the series. Each DK READER is guaranteed to capture a child's interest while developing his or her reading skills, general knowledge, and love of reading.

The five levels of DK READERS are aimed at different reading abilities, enabling you to choose the books that are exactly right for your child:

Pre-level 1: Learning to read
Level 1: Beginning to read
Level 2: Beginning to read alone
Level 3: Reading alone
Level 4: Proficient readers

The "normal" age at which a child begins to read can be anywhere from three to eight years old. Adult participation through the lower levels is very helpful for providing encouragement, discussing storylines, and sounding out unfamiliar words.

No matter which level you select, you can be sure that you are helping your child learn to read, then read to learn!

LONDON, NEW YORK, MUNICH,
MELBOURNE, AND DELHI

Editor David Fentiman
Senior Editor Helen Murray
Project Art Editor Lauren Rosier
Pre-Production Producer
Mark Staples
Producer Louise Minihane
Managing Editor Elizabeth Dowsett
Design Manager Ron Stobbart
Publishing Manager Julie Ferris
Art Director Lisa Lanzarini
Publishing Director Simon Beecroft

Reading Consultant Dr. Linda Gambrell

The LEGO© Movie screenplay by
Phil Lord and Christopher Miller

The LEGO© Movie story by
Dan Hageman & Kevin Hageman
and Phil Lord & Christopher Miller

Dorling Kindersley would like to thank Randi Sørensen
and Matthew James Ashton at the LEGO Group

First American Edition, 2014
10 9 8 7 6 5 4 3 2 1
Published in the United States by DK Publishing
4th Floor, 345 Hudson Street, New York, New York 10014

001–193756–Jan/14

Page design copyright © 2014 Dorling Kindersley Limited

DK books are available at special discounts when purchased in bulk for sales
promotions, premiums, fund-raising, or educational use.
For details, contact: DK Publishing Special Markets, 4th Floor,
345 Hudson Street, New York, New York 10014
SpecialSales@dk.com

A catalog record for this book is available
from the Library of Congress.

ISBN: 978-1-4654-1697-1 (Paperback)
ISBN: 978-1-4654-1698-8 (Hardcover)

Color reproduction in the UK by Altaimage
Printed and bound in the USA by Lake Book Manufacturing, Inc

Discover more at
www.dk.com
www.LEGO.com

Contents

JJ
EASY
LEGO

DK

BEGINNING TO READ 1

LEGO

THE LEGO MOVIE

CALLING ALL MASTER BUILDERS!

DAVID FENTIMAN

Vitruvius

This blind wizard is Vitruvius.
He is ancient and very wise.

Sparkling
cape

Vitruvius used to look after a mysterious object called the Kragle.

A powerful man called Lord Business has stolen the Kragle. He is using it in his evil plans.

Staff

Kragle

The Master Builders

Vitruvius is a Master Builder.

Master Builders have the
power to build anything they
can imagine.

The Master Builders must
hide from Lord Business and
his army of police robots.

Lord Business

Lord Business is very mean!
He plans to use the Kragle
to glue the whole
world together!

He is hunting the Master
Builders because they want
to stop his plans.

Giant————————
legs

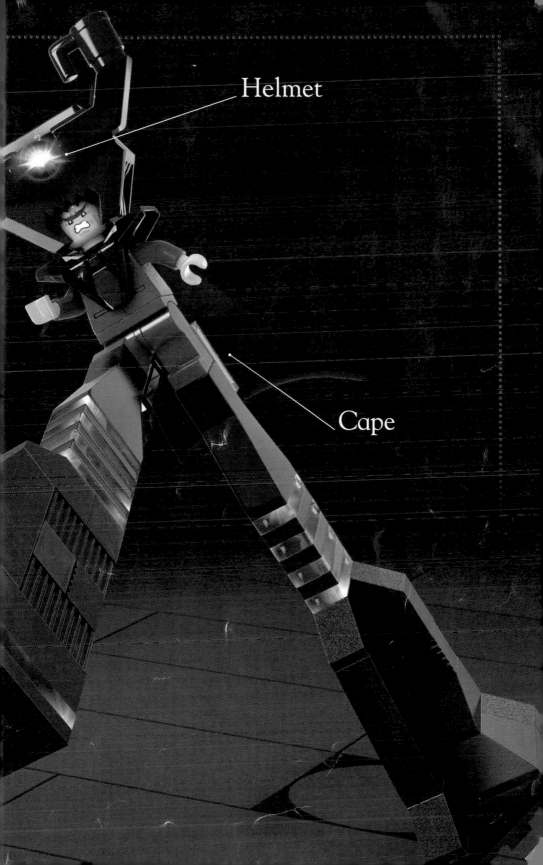

Helmet

Cape

The Special

Vitruvius said that the greatest Master Builder would rise up and defeat Lord Business.

This Master Builder would be called the Special.

Who do you think it will be?
Could it be one
of these people
from the city
of Bricksburg?

The Special

?

Amazing Builders

The Master Builders all look different. They can build all kinds of incredible things.

Punk Rocker

Let's meet some of them!

Yeti

Could one of these be the Special?

Can they help to stop Lord Business?

Artist

Hazmat Guy   Magician   Lady Liberty

Marsha   Shakespeare

Abraham
Lincoln   Circus
                       Clown

Meet Emmet

This happy man is Emmet.
He is a construction worker
who lives in Bricksburg.
Emmet always tries to
follow instructions.

He doesn't know about
Lord Business, the Master
Builders, or the
Special—yet.

Instructions

Badge

The Piece of Resistance

A mysterious object has become stuck to Emmet's back.

Piece of Resistance

It is the Piece of Resistance!
The Piece is the only thing
that can stop the Kragle.

This means that Emmet is
the Special!

Can Emmet really defeat
Lord Business?

Piece of
Resistance

Wyldstyle

Wyldstyle is one of the bravest Master Builders. She will help Emmet on his quest.

Wyldstyle is amazing at building things. She is also very good at rescuing Emmet.

Emmet thinks she is very pretty.

Sword

Batman

This is Batman.
He is Wyldstyle's boyfriend.
Batman is a super hero
and a Master Builder.

He flies a plane
called the Batwing.

He saves Wyldstyle
and Emmet when they
are in trouble.

Bat
symbol

Unikitty

Unikitty is a Master Builder. She is also princess of a magical place called Cloud Cuckoo Land.

Unikitty is half unicorn
and half kitty.

She turns into Angry Kitty
when she is very angry!

Angry Kitty

MetalBeard

MetalBeard is
a pirate and a
Master Builder.

He isn't an
ordinary pirate.
His body is made of bits of ships!

MetalBeard lost his body in a
battle against Lord Business.

Benny

Benny is a spaceman.
He likes building spaceships
more than anything else.

He is a Master Builder
so he is really good at
making spaceships.

Benny is from the 1980s.
He sometimes struggles
with new technology.

Cracked
helmet

Bad Cop

Bad Cop has been sent by Lord Business to hunt down the Master Builders.

Megaphone

He flies a Jet-Car to
look for Emmet and
the Piece of Resistance.

He wants to stop
Emmet from ruining
Lord Business's plan.

Jet-Car

Working together

Now that they know Emmet is the Special, all of the Master Builders must work together.

They must help Emmet put the Piece of Resistance on the Kragle to disarm it. Only this will defeat Lord Business— and save the world!

Glossary

Kragle
A mysterious object that can glue things.

The Special
The greatest of the Master Builders.

Piece of Resistance
The Piece fits on to the Kragle and stops it.

Angry Kitty
What Unikitty looks like when she is angry.

Jet-Car
Bad Cop's vehicle.

Index